Kindle Promotion *Made Easy*

How to promote book over Amazon Kindle
Store, make the most of the verified sales
strategies, become a marketing pro in less than
5 minutes

ISBN-13: 978-1512282993
ISBN-10: 1512282995

PRAISE FOR Kindle Promotion Made Easy

"Sourabh did an amazing job helping me publish my first ebook! He went above and beyond to answer all of my questions in getting my first book published on kindle. What a guy!"

Ryan Michael Bush
Digital Marketer, Social Media Strategist and Real Estate Investor
www.gplus.to/ryanbush

"Sourabh has been incredible in the development and moving forward with my ebook compilation project. Very educated and timely with responses and work projects. I would highly recommend him as well as work with him in the future."

Dr. James Bogash
Lifecare Chiropractic, http://lifecarechiropractic.com

"Sourabh is fast, delivers a great result and his communication is the best around - I really like working with him and look forward to our next project."

Per-Erik Persson
CEO of Notis, https://se.linkedin.com/in/coachpererik

"As usual Sourabh was GREAT. One of the best contractors on oDesk! I work with a lot of contractors and he is in the top 1%."

Adam Shepherd
CEO of Sheer Imagination, https://twitter.com/tweet4adam

MESSAGE FROM AUTHOR

You might have published a lot of books with unsatisfactory result. Or this might be your first attempt in book publishing. After doing all the hard works (eBook writing + proof-reading + formatting + cover design + compiling into Kindle friendly format + publishing) you start believing that you are done with your job and keep looking for shortcuts to promote your book. Surely it's not your fault. Most of us do think in the same way. Generally we do some common actions like the following points.

- We request nearby friends, family members to purchase our book and write some fake 5 star reviews
- We offer fellow authors / publishers to swap reviews
- We post job postings over online freelance sites and hire some part-time contractors (mostly from Asian countries) to write some fake 5 star reviews

As a result, the temporary impact might look great, because for the time being we are quite successful to confuse our audience (insisting him / her to purchase our book) with such tricky tactics.

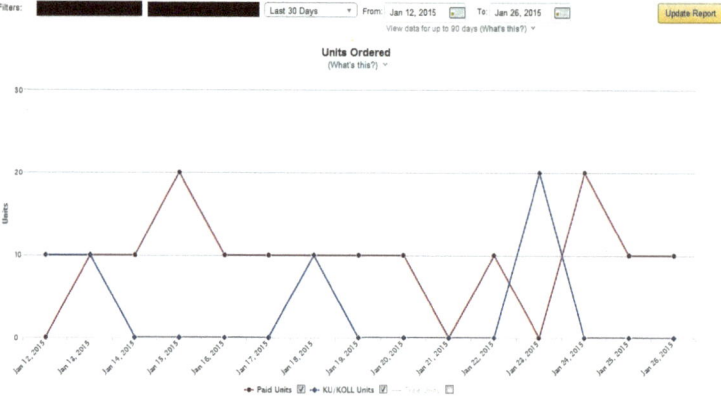

Figure 1: Temporary Impact in Sales

For long term perspective the result might become horrible. How? Well, it's pretty easy to say, because a real customer won't be either convinced or impressed with your book. As a result, your book will definitely receive consecutive 1 star reviews at a certain period of time (like the following screenshot). And from that particular moment, sales will fall down to earth in no time.

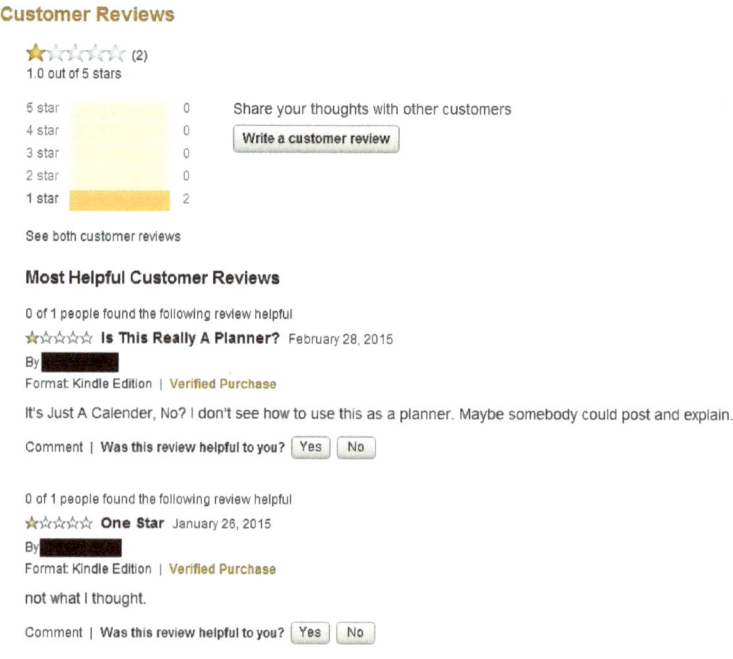

Figure 2: Long Term Impact in Customer Reviews

So, are you scared now with all these impacts?

Hey, you shouldn't have to be worried, because Kindle promotion is neither magic nor rocket science. It's just a collection of actions that can take your book to another level. All you have to do is to follow my verified suggestions (written in this book) very carefully. As I always believe to keep things simple, here I put an attempt to make it extremely simple for you.

This book is an accumulation of my 5+ years solid experience on **Kindle publishing & promotion**. On March 2015, I was recognized by oDesk as a TOP RATED FREELANCER, as I have already completed 200+ Kindle book development projects successfully (including ePub, ePub3, MOBI, KF8, Fixed-Layout, Reflowable-Layout, Paperback etc) over oDesk since last few years.

During this long period of time, I got opportunities to work with many popular authors & publishers closely via oDesk and other online freelance marketplaces. Honestly speaking, it's really very helpful to work with successful authors / publishers, because they not only share their valuable experiences, but also you can learn their strategies practically. Fortunately, you don't need to spare a lot of time like I did, because you have got my book in your hand and I have gathered every single issue that plays vital role in promoting book over KDP Store and other online stores.

Being inspired by my family-n-friends, I started to write on Amazon since last year. Here I will try to share all the verified strategies with you so that you could become a successful Kindle publisher on Amazon in a very quick time. Furthermore I love to update my latest experiences over my facebook page (https://

www.facebook.com/kindleepubebookpublishing) as always. So don't miss any point that I share with you.

Once again, my heart-felt thanks to my parents, family-n-friends and all of you for giving me a huge support to write this book for you. Let's begin the journey!

Cheers,
Sourabh Aryabhatta

IT Consultant (**Kindle, EPUB & EBOOK Publishing**)
Like My Page on Facebook: https://www.facebook.com/kindleepubebookpublishing
Connect me at LinkedIn: http://bd.linkedin.com/pub/sourabh-aryabhatta/30/4a4/8b0
Find me at Amazon: http://www.amazon.com/Sourabh-Aryabhatta/e/B00J81XNFQ

Use this book's information at your own risk.

Table of Contents

Message From Author 5

Root Cause Analysis: Why most Kindles don't sell and how you can make a big difference 11

Technical Strategies 13

Never forget to do Professional Editing & Proof-reading 13

Format, format & format your Interior book with top quality! 13

Prepare the cover image fit for kindle readers & apps 15

Specify the Table of Contents (TOC) and Start location in your book 16

Include the keywords in the metadata 17

Optimize the build size 17

KDP Publishing Strategies 19

Pick a Killer Book Title and Sub-title 19

Capitalize the Description with different approach 20

Pick the Right Category for Your Book 22

Are you missing the Right Keywords? 23

Design a Front Cover that stands differently among others ...24

Always Upload MOBI format file 25

Choose professional list prices for your book 25

Marketing Strategies..27

Make the most of Look Inside feature.............................27

Chapter Headings MUST smell like mouth-watering recipes28

Use exclusive color scheme throughout the book.................29

Become master of a particular domain............................30

Take the advantage of a free dedicated Author Page.............30

Publish your book's print version with Amazon CreateSpace 31

Create your audiobook with ACX 31

Runtime Strategies..33

Run Effective Promotional Campaign using KDP Select Program 33

Keywords, keywords and keywords! 34

Network Campaign..35

Pricing Strategies for Maximum Profit............................35

Take a break...37

Frequently asked questions...39

Recommended book by author....................................43

Notes...57

ROOT CAUSE ANALYSIS: WHY MOST KINDLES DON'T SELL AND HOW YOU CAN MAKE A BIG DIFFERENCE

Self-publishing has never been easier before. Anyone can publish a Kindle at any time and it becomes LIVE almost instantly. Hence the following reasons are responsible why a reader doesn't get attracted to a book.

- Unedited & unprofessional content
- Not proofread
- Poorly formatted
- Terrible cover design
- No **Look Inside** visibility
- Unreasonable price
- Cheap pitch in book description
- Too much advertisement
- No maintenance, update and follow-up
- Not paying attention to customer rating & feedback comments

Wow, a significant truth has been revealed by the above points. According to recent statistics, sales can be improved by **15%** (approx) if and only if you focus on story editing, copy editing and proof-reading. At the same time, an exclusive cover design can boost up earnings by at least **33%** (approx). Eventually it implies that, delivering professional content and cover page, you can immediately improve your sales by at least **48%**. Wow, that's really amazing! Isn't it?

Generally most authors don't have a background in sales, but the painful truth is that even the top quality work can fail to get attracted to readers without a complete promotional base.

Thankfully the whole process is not that much difficult that you might be worrying about. If you are really interested to explore, then you could probably make the most of the advices that my book offers. Most importantly, it will make a huge difference not only in your book's marketing, but also expand your reach to global readers beyond the Amazon store, almost immediately.

TECHNICAL STRATEGIES

NEVER FORGET TO DO PROFESSIONAL EDITING & PROOF-READING

Never publish anything without top-quality editing & proof-reading. Yes, you might be a famous author having a reputation of quality writing. You do believe that there is a very rare possibility of occurring spelling issues or grammatical errors or even fragment issues in your writing. But still you never know when that might happen to your content by either automatic flow (e.g, auto-correct feature in MS Word) or manual action (typing mistake). So the best way to avoid these issues is to spend some serious time to revise the book in a professional look.

Right! This time you will need another pair of eyes to do this job for you. May be anyone of your family members could take care of this job. Or you can trust on your closest friend, colleague or classmate. Or even you can hire some professional editor from online freelance marketplaces. It's up to your choice. But don't miss this step before moving forward to next step. After all, it's always great to fix the issues before receiving any bad comment from customers, isn't it?

FORMAT, FORMAT & FORMAT YOUR INTERIOR BOOK WITH TOP QUALITY!

Hopefully you have already got acknowledged the fact that the regular document formats (e.g, word document, pdf etc) will not work in Kindle devices as those are expected. So you will need to have some specialized Kindle friendly format.

Hmmm, you might be saying, **WAIT, I HAVE AN AMAZING FORMATTING SOLUTION**! Yes, you are right! There are lots of automated conversion tools available over internet. They are offering free conversion facilities for you assuring delivery in a few seconds. What you need to do is to just submit the input document over that website and then simply after few seconds they will prompt you with the target format. At that time you will be hoping for a good output format. Unfortunately the output result will make your face gloomy. The reason is very simple. Automated tools are good if and only if your input document is extremely plain & simple. Otherwise the outcome is nowhere near a quality work, because their internal parsers are programmed in a way that they can detect simple HTML elements only (e.g, paragraph, heading etc). But when a document contains some complicated objects (e.g, list, table, hyperlink, textbox etc), the parsers try to settle them into simple format and thus the formatting becomes really unprofessional.

Now WHAT SHOULD YOU DO? Well, you still have a lot of open options. If you have plenty of time, then you may jump into action and start learning how to develop 100% error-free mobile friendly formats, if you wish. There are lots of helping hands like hundreds of youtube videos, blogs, books (for instance, you can order my book Kindle Publishing Made Easy from Amazon store), portals etc that are ready to help you regarding this job. Still it might take some time, because at one moment, most of these methods will ultimately suggest you to learn markup languages (HTML, XHTML, XML, CSS etc) strongly. And obviously there is no shortcut technique to learn markup languages, as their volumes are growing day-by-day (already HTML5, CSS3 are available in the market).

SOUNDS TROUBLESOME? Okay, let's just forget about learning, if you don't have that much time to spend due to your own profession / business. Now what are the other alternatives? Hmmm, yes, probably we are thinking the same solution. The world has become very small with the blessings of internet and we can take help from people located at any corner of the globe.

Right, I am talking about the freelance marketplaces. Surely you will find thousands of qualified people who are always ready to help you in terms of formatting / designing / converting your content into mobile friendly formats. But be careful! Before hiring any freelancer, please check his / her profile very carefully and hire someone who is really certified, professional and able to meet the requirements 100% in due time.

PREPARE THE COVER IMAGE FIT FOR KINDLE READERS & APPS

Once you are done with the formatting of the interior book, please don't just throw a cover image by 5-minutes MS Paint operation or similar kind of drawing. Surely that will never be a professional work. According to recent statistics, an attractive cover image can improve 33% sales for a Kindle book. It's really great news indeed. But you have to make things happen, right? Before you start working with the cover image, you have to keep in mind about the following Amazon KDP Standards for cover image.

- Color profile: RGB
- Dimension: 2820x4500 px
- File Type: JPEG or TIFF
- Book title (sub-title, if any) & author name MUST be present on the cover image

Personally I do prefer JPEG more than TIFF. The reason is simple. JPEG is a more compressed format that TIFF. As a result, the final .mobi file's size is less than what it could be if the cover were a TIFF file.

Now you know the Amazon standard (required dimension, color profile and target file format). So you can begin your proceedings regarding cover page design. But how should you start? Well, if you are an expert graphics designer by yourself, then you might have started laughing, because you are ready to do it by yourself with the help of Photoshop, Illustrator etc.

On the other hand, you may hire some graphics professional who can complete this task like a piece of cake. Nevertheless, you may purchase an attractive design from various online photo-stocks as well. But at the end of the day, you MUST make sure that the cover image meets all the specified requirements.

Once the cover is ready, please just integrate it to your interior file. Then all you need to do is to test the build over your Kindle device or Kindle Previewer tool, whatever you wish.

SPECIFY THE TABLE OF CONTENTS (TOC) AND START LOCATION IN YOUR BOOK

This is purely a very simple technical work. Basically the package file (.opf) controls the sequence of the chapters (also known as **spine**) and various specific areas of a book (e.g, cover, TOC etc). Since you have to be concerned about the TOC and start location, you just need to check for the **<guide>** tag inside the .opf file. Generally it will look like the following.

```
<guide>
      <reference href="Text/cover.xhtml" title="Cover"
            type="cover" />
</guide>
```

So you will just insert two more reference items like the following.

```
<guide>
      <reference href="Text/cover.xhtml" title="Cover"
            type="cover" />
      <reference href="Text/table_of_contents.html"
            title="Table of Contents" type="toc" />
      <reference href="Text/title.html" title="Start"
  type="text" />
   </guide>
```

Where we assume that **table_of_contents.html** contains the Table of Contents of the book and **title.html** is the first page of the book.

INCLUDE THE KEYWORDS IN THE METADATA

For best search results, please include the keywords in the metadata of the book as well. To do this, you just need to add a single line inside the **<metadata>** section of the .opf file. For example, the following line can be inserted inside the <metadata> of a children book.

> <meta name="keywords" content="free download children books online, free download children's books free download children's books online, free downloadable children's books for ipad, free downloadable children's books for kindle, children books by age 1-3 childrens books by age 5-8 children books by age 6-8, childrens books by age 9 to 12 best sellers, children book collection children book sets children book series" />

OPTIMIZE THE BUILD SIZE

As we know Amazon offers two royalty schemes – (a) 35% royalty, (b) 70% royalty. For 35% royalty, your book's list price can be in between US $0.99 to US $200. On the other hand, for 70% royalty your book's list price can be in between US $2.99 to US $9.99. Let's check with the following scenario.

Assume that your book's list price is US $4.99 only. Now if you enroll your book for 35% royalty, then you will receive US $1.75 per sale. This is pretty straight-forward. But, if your book is enrolled for 70% royalty, then will you receive US $3.49 per sale?

Sorry, unfortunately the royalty calculation is not so simple for the 70% royalty scheme, because delivery cost will come into the picture immediately once you switch to 70% royalty. It directly gets applied on the list price (deducts the effective list price per sale before multiplying with the royalty) and thus affects your expected royalty per sale.

Delivery cost depends on the file-size of the .mobi file. If the file size is small, then delivery cost will be less. On the other hand, if the file size is large, then delivery cost will increase. Note that delivery cost rate is $0.1555 (approx.) per megabyte.

KDP PUBLISHING STRATEGIES

PICK A KILLER BOOK TITLE AND SUB-TITLE

It is obvious that most of the readers don't like to spend much time to read all the texts in a webpage. They scan for words and sentences exactly what they are looking for and then jump out to another one. That's why an eye-catching book title and sub-title play vital role of increasing your chances of a sale in the Amazon KDP Store. So you need to make sure that you pick the right book title and sub-title, which are simple, clear and tell the reader what your book is all about and offering straight away. For instance, let's compare the following two titles for a non-fiction technical book written to explain the procedure of Kindle publishing.

Example-1
Kindle Publishing Basics

Example-2
Kindle Publishing Made Easy: How to Format Kindle Like An Expert, How to Publish Kindle Like A Master, How to Promote Kindle Like A Pro

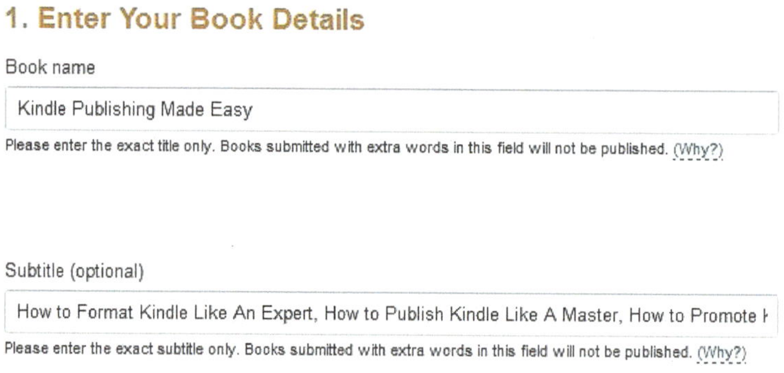

1. Enter Your Book Details

Book name

> Kindle Publishing Made Easy

Please enter the exact title only. Books submitted with extra words in this field will not be published. (Why?)

Subtitle (optional)

> How to Format Kindle Like An Expert, How to Publish Kindle Like A Master, How to Promote ꞌ

Please enter the exact subtitle only. Books submitted with extra words in this field will not be published. (Why?)

Figure 3: Book title and subtitle

The book title in example 1 is confusing. One probably could guess what the content of the book might be offering, but it isn't immediately obvious, a title about how to publish over Amazon Kindle store. The title in example 2, meanwhile, leaves no room for interpretation at all, clearly explains out what the book is all about, and attracting readers to take a closer look. The main title tells the reader what the book is all about, and the subtitle enlightens the ultimate outcome of it.

Another interesting fact is that, the sub-title covers lots of keywords and phrases like **"how to format Kindle"**, **"how to publish Kindle"** and **"how to promote Kindle"**. These phrases carry a significant value especially for readers who normally do search using those phrases. Thus your book will be always present the search result in the store at any time.

CAPITALIZE THE DESCRIPTION WITH DIFFERENT APPROACH

Book description appears in the book's Amazon page. Amazon KDP Store allows authors to write 4000 characters (maximum) for their book's description field. This is one of the areas where most of the authors fail to take advantage of their reader's mind and lose sales. So it is very much crucial how you can make the most of this limited number of characters and increase your book's sales.

Pitching generic advertising words like **Great News!** or **Good News!** won't help a big deal here, because this strategy has become very old and readers won't get attracted by those kinds of cheap words. You just need to sense reader's pulse what exactly he / she is looking for.

Please note that description will surely vary depending on the type of your book (e.g, children book, recipe book, fitness book etc). But it is imperative that you MUST cover as many characters as you can. May be some early praise or positive testimonial or short outline of story characters can be helpful.

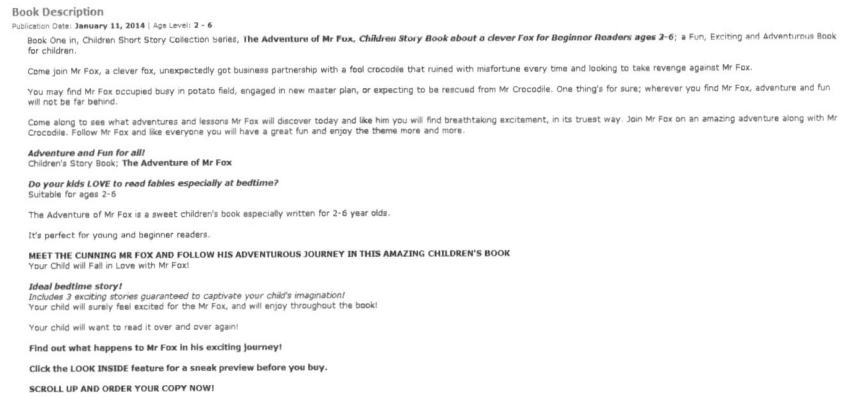

Figure 4: Sample description for children book

Formatted texts (having bold, italic styles, bullet points) are useful to grab reader's attention. So the **Author Central** area will be very handy to place that formatted text, because normal **Description** field (in KDP store) doesn't allow formatted text.

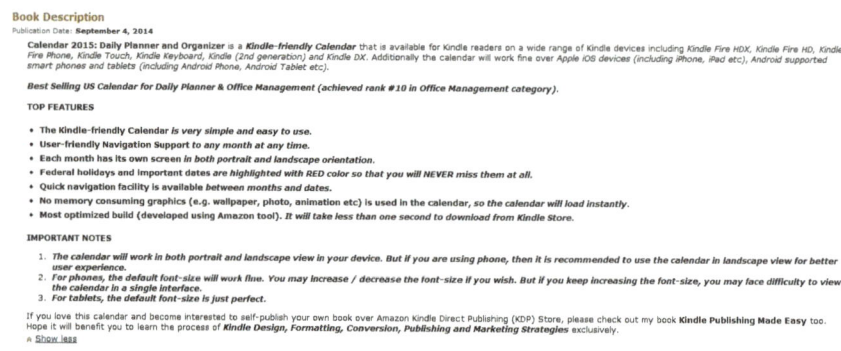

Figure 5: Sample description for calendar book

PICK THE RIGHT CATEGORY FOR YOUR BOOK

When you will be uploading your book over Amazon KDP Store, Amazon will allow you to pick two categories (maximum) for your book. So you need to think very carefully about the two categories that your book fits most.

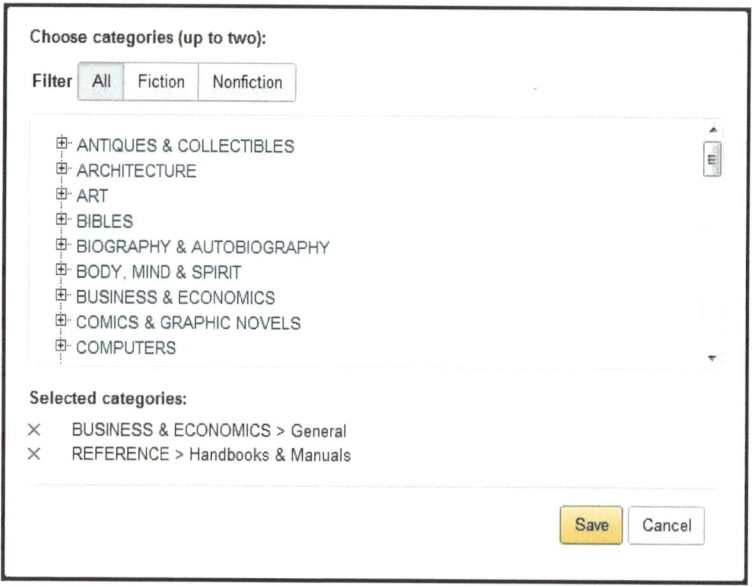

Figure 6: Available categories in Amazon KDP Store

Many new authors often do a mistake by choosing inaccurate

categories. As a result, expected sales are not achieved and all the hard work goes in vain.

Amazon offers hundreds of sub-categories to choose from the KDP Store, so it may be wise to experiment with placing the book in several (similar) different categories over time, to observe which brings more sales.

ARE YOU MISSING THE RIGHT KEYWORDS?

Keywords are actual search terms that people enter into the search engines when conducting a search. In order to achieve better rankings in search engines, you MUST have to spend a good amount of time for keywords research (http://en.wikipedia.org/wiki/Keyword_research) to pick the right keywords for your book. Undoubtedly it is one of the golden opportunities that most of the newbie authors miss frequently.

For instance, let me tell you a real story. Few months ago, I got an opportunity to work with a new author. He was a very good badminton player having great writing skill as well. He asked me to help him regarding his book's Kindle formatting & publishing over KDP Store. I happily agreed to help him. During the development time, I read few random pages in some quick glance. His content was surely amazing and the cover page was simply outstanding. While he was uploading the book over KDP Store by sharing screen, unfortunately I noticed that he wrote only 7 distinct words as keywords in the **Search Keywords** field. It was really unbelievable, because people rarely search using those kinds of single keywords. Thus a quality work might fall short due to missing right keywords.

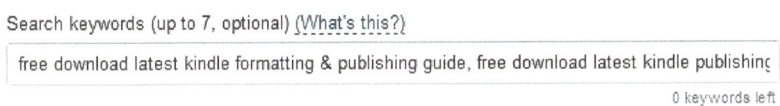

Figure 7: Sample search keywords

There are several keyword research tools over internet that can meet your demand. For example, Google AdWords Keyword planner, Google traffic estimator, Google Trends etc. What they simply do is as follows.

- Get traffic estimates for the target keyword.
- Generate new keywords by combining different keyword lists
- Create new keyword variations based on initial keyword

DESIGN A FRONT COVER THAT STANDS DIFFERENTLY AMONG OTHERS

I don't really understand why most of the new authors never realize the importance of an attractive cover page. Probably they think that reader will read the book, not the cover. Literally their statement is correct, but insignificant in the perspective of sales. Well, the issue is very simple. Thousands of customers are looking for their desired books over Amazon store. When they search with certain keywords, they find a list of similar books in same genre. Now, let's think about such a scenario where you can see a list of similar books with almost same price and same number of reviews. According to human's natural instinct, you will definitely pick the book having eye-catching cover image on it. That's absolutely correct! Because almost 33% of customers click on the **Buy now with 1-Click** button almost instantly, because they know this product might get out-of-stock in no time.

Figure 8: Front cover

Here comes the point. So you MUST create the cover irresistible to buyers, because it's the first impression that makes your book different from others. If you design a plain cover, then still a few people will notice your book, but unfortunately most of the readers will ignore your book and move to the next one.

ALWAYS UPLOAD MOBI FORMAT FILE

Yes, Amazon KDP Store allows uploading word document (doc, docx, odt etc), html, epub and many other format files, but the formatting is NOT 100% guaranteed in all these format files. Surely you will be expecting to see the formatting as close as possible in the output Kindle friendly format. Only .mobi format can guarantee you to meet that quality.

CHOOSE PROFESSIONAL LIST PRICES FOR YOUR BOOK

Undoubtedly you are looking to publish your book over all territories to reach as many audiences as possible. So it is recommended that you should choose professional list prices for your book over all the Amazon stores. For all the Amazon stores (except Amazon US Store), there is an option of setting price based on US price. You should not tick that checkbox. The reason is that it will automatically set some unprofessional list price calculating the currency conversion rate. Please see the following figure for details.

	List Price	Royalty Rate	Delivery Costs	Estimated Royalty
Amazon.com	$ 3.99 USD Price must be between $0.99 and $200.00	35%	n/a	$1.40
Amazon.co.uk	☑ Set UK price automatically based on US price £2.63 (£2.19 without UK VAT)	35%	n/a	£0.77*
Amazon.de	☑ Set DE price automatically based on US price €3.56 (€2.99 without DE VAT)	35%	n/a	€1.05*
Amazon.fr	☑ Set FR price automatically based on US price €3.56 (€3.37 without FR VAT)	35%	n/a	€1.18*

Figure 9: Unprofessional list price over UK, DE, FR Store

To avoid automatic unprofessional list price, please uncheck all these tick marks from the checkboxes and then use some list price that looks professional and seems close to US list price (considering currency conversion rate). For example, for the above case, you could pick 2.95 GBP for the UK Store and 3.95 EURO for the DE and FR Stores.

MARKETING STRATEGIES

MAKE THE MOST OF LOOK INSIDE FEATURE

Before purchasing any product, a smart customer always takes a careful look at it. And if that product is a book, then he / she will definitely try to examine as many pages as he / she can. Amazon KDP Store offers this exclusive feature to customers, which is also known as **Look Inside** feature. It helps readers to see the first 10% content of the book for free!

Look Inside really plays a very important role in customer's mind whether to purchase the book or not. PLEASE NOTE! **Look Inside** feature works for the 100% flowable format Kindle (also known as reflowable format) only. That's why it is strongly recommended that you *should* develop your Kindle as reflowable Kindle to utilize this feature completely.

Figure 10: Look Inside feature

Now you are well acknowledged about the fact that the first 10% of the book MUST be very special and engaging, so that it becomes successful to capture customer's attention fully on your book. Obviously the whole content is very important, but the first

10% content WILL make the instant impression in customer's mind. While a customer is reading your book using the Look Inside feature, can be considered as the decision-making time. So you MUST be very careful what you have written at the beginning of the book. It is strongly recommended that a *click-able Table of Contents* should be placed at the very beginning of the book (right after the Copyright Page). Its primary goal is to let the reader check the headings and make him / her impressed with your content.

CHAPTER HEADINGS MUST SMELL LIKE MOUTH-WATERING RECIPES

You might ask me, "Why should I give importance on chapter headings? I have my contents well organized for readers." Well, it's a long story, so let me explain please. As I have already said, customer should be able to see the click-able Table of Contents at the very beginning of the book through the **Look Inside** feature. Since Table of Contents is generated by the headings & sub-headings of the book, so a customer is able to view them very comfortably. Now the outcome could be either optimistic or pessimistic.

If the headings & sub-headings sound great, then reader will become more interested to discover the internal message of that particular section(s). Thus probability of sales will certainly increase without any doubt. On the other hand, if the chapter headings are poor, customers won't get attracted to purchase your book. They will simply reject your book and jump away, once they find the headings ambiguous & low-quality.

In a summary, it will be really a big mistake if you don't spend much time in writing appropriate chapter heading for each of the sections & chapters. The best way of writing a chapter heading is to use correct keywords that can represent the target section's content clearly.

USE EXCLUSIVE COLOR SCHEME THROUGHOUT THE BOOK

If you want to establish yourself in eBook business, then you MUST have to understand your reader's mind. A reader will not only read the content, but also notice the color scheme of your book. Variation of colors always carries special meaning and takes a book to another level. How? Let me explain please. When you notice some text in either bold or italic or underline, definitely your eyes do concentrate more on that sentence. Similarly when you do notice some change in text color in any section, you do understand that this particular section contains some important message for you.

So it is highly recommended that you should use some exclusive color scheme throughout your book. It will not only keep the audience super-engaged, but also make the look-n-feel different from other books. Now question might be asked like "**how can I pick a color scheme?**" or "**what should be the best color scheme for my book?**" right? Yes, we have some good solution. You might be running some other business via your own website. Or you might be promoting your own brand or product via some other medium. Then why don't you make that color scheme exclusively available in your book? Right, that's what I was trying to point about. You can easily promote your own brand or product or service throughout the book by picking that particular color scheme or theme wherever necessary.

For example, say you do run a yoga training institute and sell some exclusive services there. You have your own company logo, slogan and promotional message. Then you can easily pick that theme (your logo, slogan, promotional message, color scheme etc) throughout your yoga learning book. It's really pretty simple and definitely will help to grow both businesses in this hand-shaking protocol. It means, if somebody purchases that book, then he / she will know about your yoga institute. On the other hand, it will be easier for you to share your book with your existing audience (for example, yoga learners in your institute), because they can verify easily that you are the author of this book.

BECOME MASTER OF A PARTICULAR DOMAIN

There is an old proverb, "Jack of all trades master of none". It means, if you try to become guru of every single domain, then at the end of the day you will not have expertise on any single area. So as an emerging author, you should not try to write on any topic you wish. You might disagree with me. But statistics will stand against you. The reason is very simple. People will like to read your book, because they know you are writing in a single domain. Once they will discover that you are trying to appear in different domains, they might not take it positively unless you are unbelievably popular in the eBook publishing world. So if you are a famous author, then it's a different story. But if you are a new author, then you should approach forward very carefully.

Suppose you are a recipe expert. People see your recipe books available on the online stores. So you should try to grow your business in the domain of recipe books. Now at the same time if you try to appear in children book, then many people will put question mark on your writing skill and quality, because there is no match in between a recipe book and a children book. Yes, technically there might be some similarities, but in a bigger picture there is rarely any match in between them. So surely audience will reject your book and your existing customers will disappear from your book immediately.

TAKE THE ADVANTAGE OF A FREE DEDICATED AUTHOR PAGE

Author Central is a free effective service (powered by Amazon) that helps to share an author's most up-to-date information with customers. It is a very handy place to introduce your books to your customers. On the author page, you can add essential information about you—including bibliographies, biographies, your photos, and even feeds to blog posts. It really helps you to boost your sales potential on Amazon. Normally it takes 3 to 5 days for the Author Page to appear on the Amazon.com site.

To learn more, visit the following link. https://authorcentral. amazon.com/

PUBLISH YOUR BOOK'S PRINT VERSION WITH AMAZON CREATESPACE

Self publishing has never been easier before. Amazon's CreateSpace platform (https://www.createspace.com/) gives you an amazing opportunity to publish the print edition of your book seamlessly. You can use free CreateSpace templates (https://www. createspace.com/en/community/docs/DOC-1323) to organize the book by yourself. Or you can take help from professional publishing services from different sources as well. Here you will have control of your work and can make your book's paperback version available to millions of readers worldwide on Amazon. com and other distribution channels. Another interesting thing is that, once you publish over Amazon CreateSpace, it automatically links up with its Kindle version and vice versa.

CREATE YOUR AUDIOBOOK WITH ACX

The Audiobook Creation Exchange (ACX) (http://www.acx.com/) is another Amazon platform that helps to turn your book into an audiobook and creates an opportunity to generate more revenue. It will connect you with professional audio producers to create audiobooks.

RUNTIME STRATEGIES

RUN EFFECTIVE PROMOTIONAL CAMPAIGN USING KDP SELECT PROGRAM

If you are new to Kindle publishing then I am very glad to let you know that Amazon KDP provides various exclusive opportunities to promote your book for free. Wow, it's really amazing, isn't it? :) When you move forward to publish your book over KDP Store, Amazon offers you to enroll your book for **KDP Select Program**. If you are a newbie, then KDP Select Program will surely be a great option for you to promote your book in a quick time.

By the way, when you choose **KDP Select** for your book, you're committing to make the digital format available exclusively through KDP during the entirety of its enrollment in the program. It means your book (enrolled with KDP Select) cannot be available for free or for purchase in digital format anywhere else, including publishing the content of your book on the web, including on your own website, blog, etc. To know more about KDP Select Program, please visit here (https://kdp.amazon.com/help?topicId=A6KILDRNSCOBA).

KDP Select Program offers two exclusive promotional campaigns – **Free Book Promotions** and **Kindle Countdown Deals**.

Free Book Promotions – It will offer your book free to readers for up to five days at your discretion during each 90-day enrollment period in KDP Select. To know more about Free Book Promotions, please visit here (https://kdp.amazon.com/help?topicId=A34IQ0W14ZKXM9).

Kindle Countdown Deals – It will allow customers to purchase your book for a promotional price (obviously less than regular price) for a certain period of time. Customers can see the regular price and the promotional price on the book's detail page, as well as a countdown clock telling them how much time is left at the promotional price. To know more about Kindle Countdown Deals, please click here (https://kdp.amazon.com/help?topicId=A2MJTCAYTCBNW2).

When to run a Free Promotion?

Many experts agree that Saturday and Sunday are the best days for running free promotional campaign. The fact is that these two days are weekends when people love to spend their time on websites to taste free books. So you should not forget about the federal holidays as well. If you are planning to release your book very soon, then please visit here (http://www.amazon.com/Calendar-2015-Sourabh-Aryabhatta-ebook/dp/B00NBJ2JRE) to check the federal holidays and important dates of upcoming year.

KEYWORDS, KEYWORDS AND KEYWORDS!

Let's think about a simple scenario. You have written a quality book and published over Amazon Kindle Store. You did all the hard work and waiting to see the result. A few copies were sold in first couple of days. But after a few days you are not observing any single sale of your book. It really sounds terrible, isn't it? But unfortunately it happens for most of the newbie authors who don't give importance on a periodic task. Yes, you are right! I am talking about **SEO**. SEO stands for Search Engine Optimization. You can easily do some simple SEO work by using the **Search** textbox in Amazon's page.

NETWORK CAMPAIGN

It will be undoubtedly a terrible mistake if you don't run promotional campaign across the popular networks (facebook, twitter, google+, linkedin, instagram, pinterest etc) periodically. It's just a simple technique of spreading the good news across your networks. It will engage people to your books effectively, if you run free promotion at the same time.

PRICING STRATEGIES FOR MAXIMUM PROFIT

It has been always a burning question - "**How should I price my Kindle book?**" Well, Amazon KDP Store provides a service called **KDP Pricing Support (Beta)** that suggests a reasonable price based on historic data of similar kind of books.

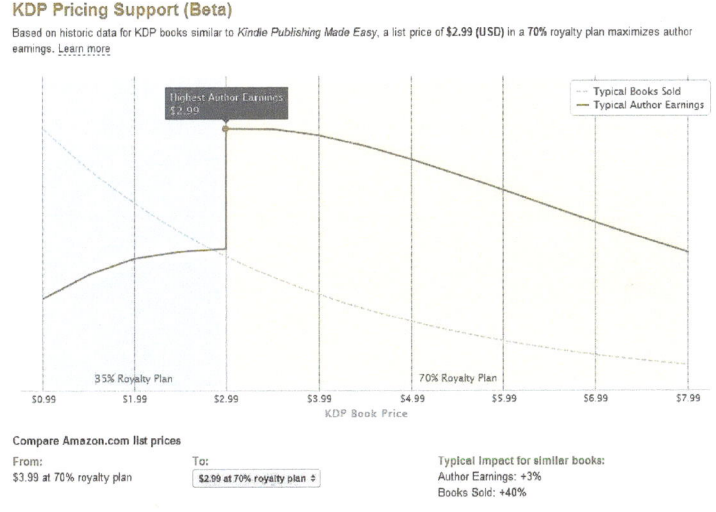

Figure 11: KDP Pricing Support (Beta)

But you might not agree with its result every time, because it analyzes list price based on statistical data, not strategically. KDP allows you to pick either 70% "royalty" (aka: profit per eBook sale) or 35%. The catch is, to make 70% you MUST price your book competitively—between $2.99 and $9.99. The lowest price of $2.99 keeps the content from being devalued, while keeping it at a no-brainer investment for customers. Anything lower than $2.99 and many reader will begin to wonder if the content inside is worth it, unless the description of the book states the book is unusually short (30-60 pages).

So why would anyone pick a price outside that magical range of higher profit boundaries? The reason is that, *sometimes the content demands it*.

Strategically we can divide all the Kindle books into several categories. I will try to explain few of them in the following sections.

Lead Generation

Short Kindle books are often known as lead generating books, containing powerful bursts of information. These books are typically **priced in between $0.99 and $2.99**, due to their shorter length and ability to capture people onto the author's list for future follow up. Lead-generating eBooks are mostly designed to entice the customer to visit a website for an extra free goodie—typically something only available to Kindle readers.

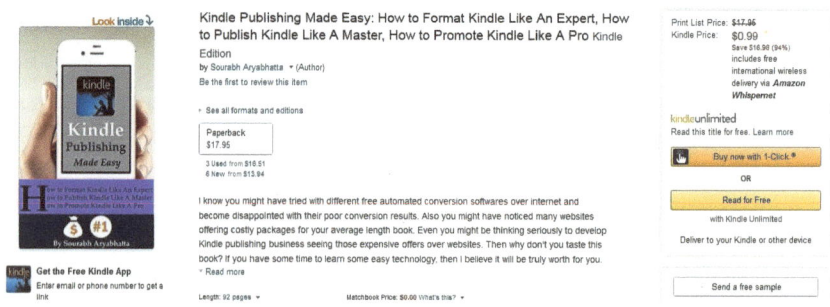

Figure 12: Lead Generating Book

Core Content

Core content books are meant to be read, devoured, notated and referenced. Mostly you will see this type of books in the business category of a bookstore. Life-cycle of these books typically starts from paperback version (Amazon CreateSpace), and then released in eBook format (Amazon KDP Store). People buy this kind of books to learn as much as they can about a specific topic. They include a lot of things than just the main points about a topic.

These eBooks are priced in between $2.99 and $9.99. Core content books are naturally considered as "trade" titles—mainstream topics that might face a lot of competition, but sell significantly anyway as each book covers parts of topics not covered by other books on the same subject.

Specialty Books

Textbooks and niche books (on specific topics like Object-oriented programming etc) are known as specialty books. These eBooks are priced at $14.99 or even higher. The tighter the niche, the harder it is to find quality information about the topic, so the higher the price can be. I've even noticed some specialty eBooks selling for almost $200. At those prices, a 35% KDP royalty is not bad compared to 70% royalty of a $9.99 book.

Fiction

Fiction book's price completely depends on the reputation of the author. For newbie unknown authors / first-time authors, it is recommended that your fiction books should be priced closer to $2.99. For reputed authors (having a solid audience and thousands of followers), a higher price closer to $9.99 will work.

TAKE A BREAK

I guess you might be finding every phase somehow a bit difficult to remember, right? Wait, let's take some break. Please don't become hopeless to see all these techniques comparing with your current progress. You are doing absolutely fine. So don't panic please. All you need to do is to follow these verified strategies one-by-one in a smooth way. Yes, you may miss one or two or may be more points. But the fact is that you are in the right track. Kindle publishing and promotion is NEVER a one-time task. You need to stay tuned with your book very carefully. You have to keep your eyes open in KDP Store's Report page, analyze market demand (see what are the latest trends), spread your book's news over social networks, update your book on regular basis (may be twice a month) and keep researching on the best keywords.

FREQUENTLY ASKED QUESTIONS

I have published my book over KDP Store a couple of weeks ago. Still I am not observing any significant sales. What should I do now?

Please check all the strategies described in this book very carefully and then try to apply them if you have missed any of these techniques. Hopefully you will notice effective change in your sales very soon.

I have read a lot of articles on Kindle promotion, but unable to figure out the exact way that helps. Can you tell me what should be the ultimate promotional strategy for a Kindle book?

In a summary, it needs to be very organized about the plan of promotional campaign. The whole process needs to be divided into three phases: Pre-release, LIVE, Post-release.

Pre-release: High-demand niche, great eye-catching cover, intriguing title, great content and usage of correct keywords.

LIVE: KDP Select, Strategic Free Giveaway (for a limited period), Great Exposure to people through social & business networks, blogs, forums, communities.

Post-release: Update your book (to place a link for requesting the reader for review), check & update keywords (if needed), release paperback & audio version.

I want to self-publish my book over KDP Store. But I cannot determine the list price for my book. It's a fiction book. Can you please help?

Please check the **"PRICING STRATEGIES FOR MAXIMUM PROFIT"** section of this book. Under this section, you will find the pricing strategies of fiction books.

I am going to self-publish my graphics-heavy children book over KDP Store. All the technical works are done by my Kindle designer. But I am worries about its file size. When I upload it over KDP Store, it's about 20 MB approx. I don't want to bear this high delivery cost. How can I optimize the file-size of my book?

✓ Compress the pictures for "Web/Screen" inside your word document.

✓ To generate HTML file, please use Microsoft Office instead of any other word processor (like OpenOffice) and then use the option "Web Page, Filtered"

✓ You should remove the unnecessary media file, CSS class, HTML file etc from your source package (if any).

✓ For cover image, use medium quality JPG file, instead of PNG file.

I am in a process of self-publishing my recipe book over KDP Store. I want to make sure that the recipe photos do NOT lose any picture quality and placed correctly in the book. How do I do that?

Please make sure that your photos meet the following specification.

✓ RGB color profile is used for the photos
✓ Either JPG or PNG format is used in the book
✓ At least 300 DPI
✓ Lossless compression algorithm is applied once converted

into mobile friendly format
✓ Occupied with maximum dimension

I have published a self-help book over KDP Store few days ago. Now I want to update my book with several links and information. Is there any easy way to do that?

Sorry, unfortunately there is no shortcut way to do this job. The best way will be to use the source code of existing MOBI file and update necessary HTML split file and finally compress it again into MOBI. Once everything is done, you can simply re-upload it over KDP Store. It won't take much time to update the existing Kindle book.

I have updated my existing Kindle book's cover image. But it is still now showing at "Look Inside" area. What is wrong here?

There is nothing wrong with the Look Inside feature. Sometimes it takes 2-3 business days to update the Look Inside area of a book over KDP Store.

RECOMMENDED BOOK BY AUTHOR

Kindle Publishing Made Easy reveals the ultimate secrets in Kindle Formatting and Publishing exclusively. If you're a first-time Kindle publisher or technologically challenged then this book is just for you! It will immediately benefit your Kindle formatting skill in just minutes per day.

Kindle Publishing Made Easy
(http://www.amazon.com/Kindle-Publishing-Made-Easy-Publish-ebook/dp/B00QJKUMEY)

Top Features

- ✓ You can easily get familiarized with fundamental Kindle terminologies (with necessary pictures)

- ✓ How to format a book for Kindle in a comfortable step-by-step technique (with necessary screenshots)

- ✓ How to control the user-friendly features (like NCX View Navigation) effortlessly

- ✓ You can learn the ultimate mechanism of creating compatible Kindle Format 8 (KF8) build for all generation Kindle devices and Kindle apps

- ✓ How to improve your book's ranking, get reviews, and encourage sales using verified marketing strategies

Don't miss the opportunity to taste this book! Buy your copy and start the journey in the world of Kindle Publishing!